Magnets

by Becky Olien

Consultant:
Philip W. Hammer, Ph.D.
Vice President, The Franklin Center
The Franklin Institute Science Museum

Bridgestone Books
an imprint of Capstone Press
esota

Bridgestone Books are published by Capstone Press
151 Good Counsel Drive, P.O. Box 669, Mankato, Minnesota 56002
http://www.capstone-press.com

Library of Congress Cataloging-in-Publication Data
Olien, Rebecca.
     Magnets / by Becky Olien.
     p. cm.—(Our physical world)
     Includes bibliographical references and index.
     ISBN 0-7368-1406-X (hardcover)
     1. Magnets—Juvenile literature. 2. Magnetism—Juvenile literature. [1. Magnets.
2. Magnetism.] I. Title. II. Series.
QC753.7 .O45 2003
538'.4—dc21   2001007889

Summary: Introduces magnetism, and provides instructions for an activity to demonstrate
     some of its characteristics.

Editorial Credits

Erika Mikkelson, editor; Karen Risch, product planning editor; Linda Clavel, designer and
     illustrator; Alta Schaffer, photo researcher; Nancy White, photo stylist

Photo Credits

Capstone Press/Gary Sundermeyer, cover, 4–5, 7, 8, 17; Jim Foell, 9, 14, 15
Hulton/Archive Photos by Getty Images, 21
Photri-Microstock/Mark E. Gibson, 13
Visuals Unlimited/David Wrobel, 12; Gerald & Buff Corsi, 16; Arthur R. Hill, 19

1 2 3 4 5 6 07 06 05 04 03 02

Table of Contents

Magnetism

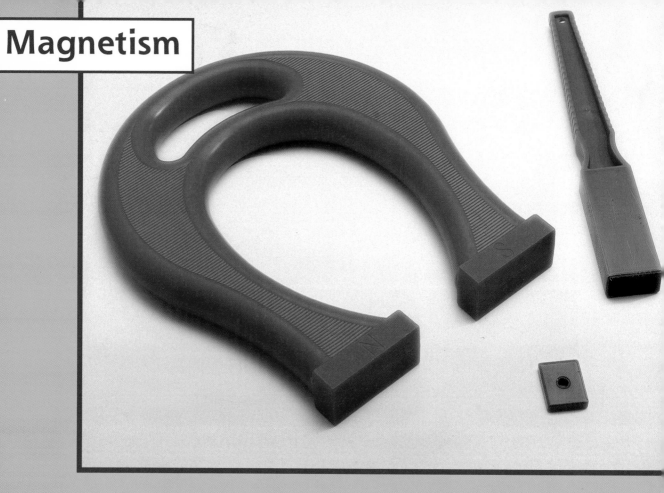

Magnetism is a form of energy. Magnetism makes some metal objects jump, spin, or stick to other metals.

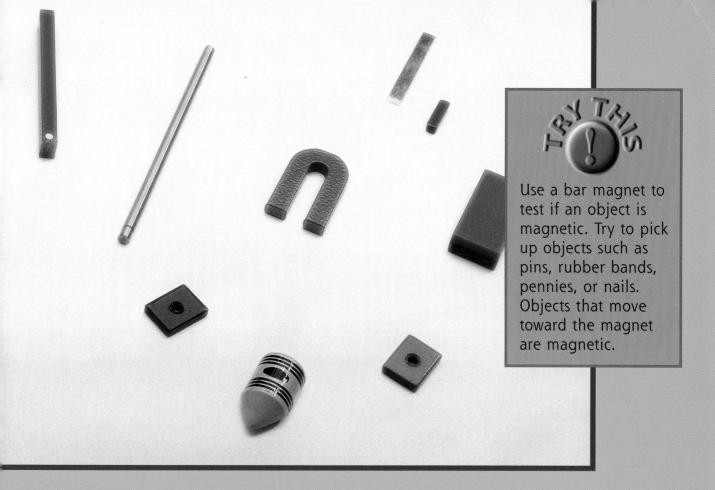

TRY THIS

!

Use a bar magnet to test if an object is magnetic. Try to pick up objects such as pins, rubber bands, pennies, or nails. Objects that move toward the magnet are magnetic.

Many metals are magnetic. Magnets are different shapes, sizes, and strengths. Some magnets are bar or horseshoe shapes.

energy
the ability to move things or do work

5

How Magnets Work

Magnets only move objects made from iron, steel, nickel, or cobalt. Most paper clips and nails contain iron. These objects jump and stick when a magnet gets close. Magnets do not attract all metal objects. A magnet will not pick up aluminum foil or a penny.

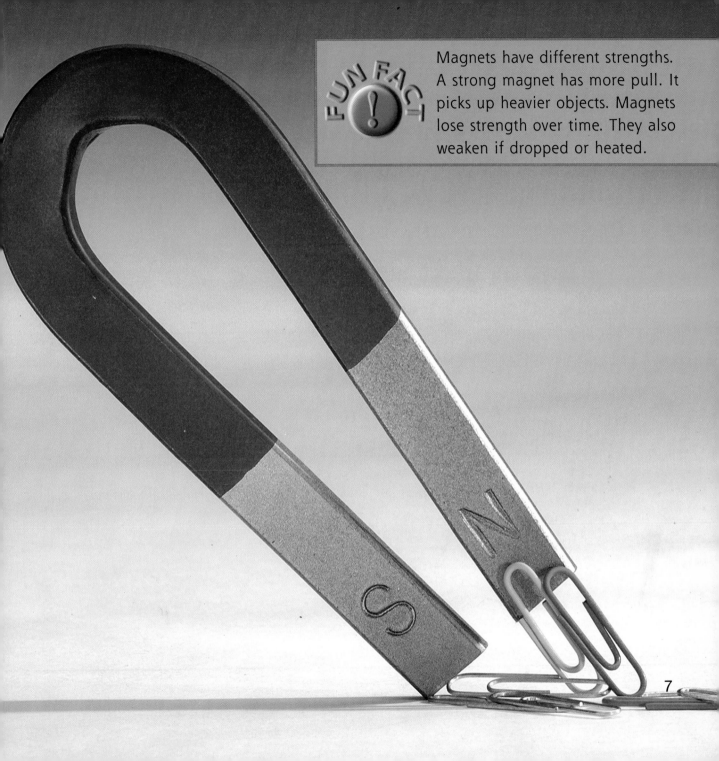

Magnets have different strengths. A strong magnet has more pull. It picks up heavier objects. Magnets lose strength over time. They also weaken if dropped or heated.

N

S

Magnetic Field

A magnetic field surrounds a magnet. This area pulls in magnetic objects. The magnetic field is strongest at a magnet's north and south pole.

TRY THIS

Place two bar magnets end to end. Do they stick together? Turn one magnet around. Now do they stick together?

North and south poles attract each other. These poles stick together. Magnets repel when two north or south poles are near each other.

pole
the end of a magnet

9

Earth Is a Magnet

Earth is a giant magnet. Deep inside Earth is a core of metal. Liquid iron in the outer core makes Earth's magnetic field. Earth has a north pole and a south pole like a magnet does. A magnet hanging by a string turns to line up with Earth's magnetic poles.

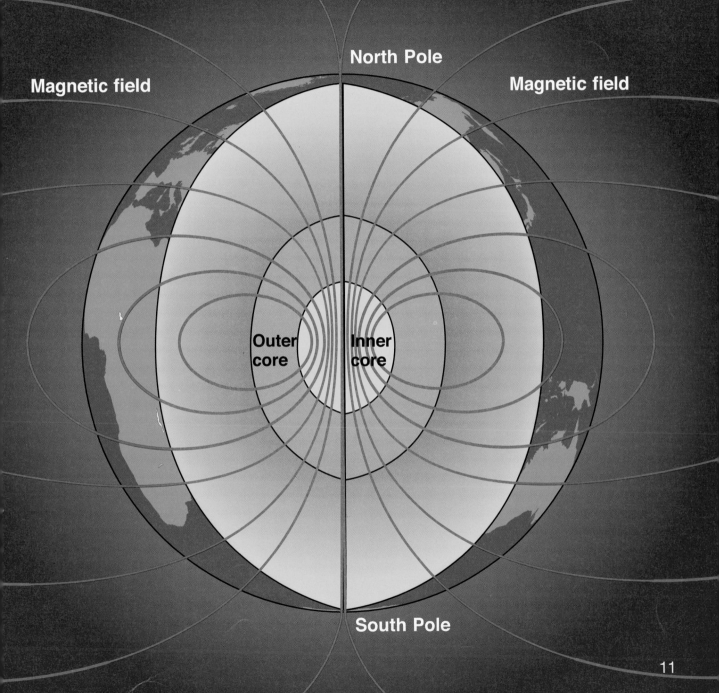

The Compass

A compass tells people which direction is north. It has a magnetic needle. The needle lines up with Earth's magnetic poles.

The compass needle points north even
when the compass is turned. Airplane
pilots and hikers use compasses.

Making Magnets

TRY THIS !

Use a strong magnet to rub a nail many times in the same direction. Now try to pick up a paper clip with the nail.

People use magnets to make new magnets. A nail touching a magnet picks up a paper clip. The nail only is magnetic when touching the magnet.

A nail becomes a magnet by rubbing it with another magnet. The nail now can pick up paper clips without touching another magnet.

Using Magnets

Magnets are useful. Cupboard doors
stay closed with magnets. Computers
use magnets to store information.

magnet inside
a computer

16

Electric motors use magnets to turn. A fan
has an electric motor. Magnetic tape is
used to record sounds or pictures.

Electromagnets

Electromagnets are made with electricity. An electromagnet is made by wrapping wire around a nail. The wire's ends connect to a battery. The nail can pick up paper clips when the wires touch the battery. Cranes use huge electromagnets to pick up heavy pieces of metal.

Michael Faraday

English scientist Michael Faraday discovered how to use magnets to make electricity. In 1831, he invented the electric generator. This machine uses a spinning magnet to make electricity. Today, power plants use generators to make large amounts of electricity.

21

Hands On: Magnet Mover

Magnets move things made of steel. This activity will show you how magnetism works through paper and water.

What You Need

1½-inch (4-centimeter) square of thin green plastic
Scissors
Stapler
Large paper cup
Water
Magnet

What You Do

1. Cut out a turtle shape from the plastic.
2. Use the stapler to put one staple in the middle of the plastic.
3. Fill a paper cup half full with water.
4. Gently lay the turtle in the water so it floats.
5. Hold the cup in one hand. Drag a magnet on the outside of the cup to move the turtle.
6. Can you make your turtle move forward and backward? Try using the magnet to make your turtle spin. Drag the magnet down the side of the cup to make your turtle dive. Drag the magnet up the cup to make the turtle climb out of the water.

What other ways can you move your turtle with a magnet? If your turtle does not move, use a stronger magnet or less water.

Words to Know

attract (uh-TRAKT)—when two objects pull together; a magnet attracts iron.

battery (BAT-uh-ree)—a container with chemicals that make electricity

electricity (e-lek-TRISS-uh-tee)—a form of energy used to run machines and to make heat and light

generator (JEN-uh-ray-tur)—a machine that uses a spinning magnet to make electricity

magnetic field (mag-NET-ik FEELD)—the area around a magnet that has the power to attract magnetic metals

magnetic pole (mag-NET-ik POHL)—the ends of a magnet where magnetism is strongest

repel (ri-PEL)—to push apart; like poles of magnets repel each other.

Read More

Bocknek, Jonathan. *The Science of Magnets.* Living Science. Milwaukee: Gareth Stevens, 2000.

Flaherty, Michael. *Magnetism and Magnets.* Science Factory. Brookfield, Conn.: Copper Beech Books, 1999.

Hunter, Rebecca. *Electricity and Magnetism.* Discovering Science. Austin, Texas: Raintree Steck-Vaughn, 2001.

Internet Sites

BrainPOP—Magnetism
http://www.brainpop.com/science/forces/magnetism/
index.weml
Canada Science and Technology Museum—Magnets
http://www.science-tech.nmstc.ca/english/schoolzone/
Info_Magnets.cfm
Exploratorium Science Snacks—Snacks about Magnetism
http://www.exploratorium.edu/snacks/iconmagnetism.html

Index